THE STORY
OF Heaven

Resources for *The Story*

Books

The Story

The Story for Teens

The Story for Kids

The Story for Children, a Storybook Bible

The Heart of the Story (by Randy Frazee)

Exploring the Story (by Adam Barr)

Curriculum

The Story Adult Curriculum Participant's Guide and DVD

The Story of Heaven Study Guide and DVD

The Story of Jesus Participant's Guide and DVD

The Story of Jesus Teen Curriculum DVD

The Story for Kids: Later Elementary Curriculum CD-ROM

The Story for Children: Early Elementary Curriculum CD-ROM

The Story for Little Ones: Preschool Curriculum CD-ROM

The Story of Jesus for Kids Curriculum

Other

The Story Implementation Guide

The Story Church Resource DVD

Study Guide   Three Sessions

THE STORY
OF *Heaven*

EXPLORING THE HOPE AND PROMISE OF ETERNITY

MAX LUCADO &
RANDY FRAZEE

ZONDERVAN®

ZONDERVAN

The Story of Heaven Study Guide
Copyright © 2014 by Max Lucado and Randy Frazee

This title is also available as a Zondervan ebook.
Visit www.zondervan.com/ebooks.

Requests for information should be addressed to:

Zondervan, 3900 Sparks Dr., Grand Rapids, Michigan 49546

ISBN 978-0-310-82027-7

Cover photography: Thinkstock
Interior design: Beth Shagene

Printed in the United States of America

14 15 16 17 18 19 /DCI/ 21 20 19 18 17 16 15 14 13 12 11 10 9 8 7 6 5 4 3 2 1

Contents

Introduction

THE STORY OF HEAVEN STUDY GUIDE COMBINES CONTENT from two well-loved pastors and authors — Max Lucado (*God's Story, Your Story*) and Randy Frazee (*The Story*) — along with brand-new material to provide solid, biblical teaching on heaven and life after death. Designed for use with *The Story of Heaven* video, it's a timely study for small groups, churches, and individuals.

Using This Study Guide

- Each session of this book consists of Bible Readings from the New International Version (NIV) followed by a study guide that includes space for taking notes while viewing the video teaching, group discussion questions, prayer cues, and personal application ideas for between meetings.

- Ideally, with the exception of session 1, you will read the Bible Readings *before* your group meets so that you are prepared to jump right into the video presentation. However, even if you have not had opportunity to read the Bible Readings ahead of time, please attend the group anyway—the discussion questions typically focus on shorter portions of these same Bible passages, which you will read during the session itself.

- As you use the study guide and listen to Max or Randy's video teaching, you will occasionally encounter the terms **Upper Story** and **Lower Story**. What do they mean?

All through the story of the Bible two parallel and beautiful dramas unfold: There is the **Upper Story**. God is real, he is present, and he is working on our behalf. Heaven is breaking into the world more than we recognize, and the story of God's seeking love, perpetual grace, and longing for relationship with ordinary people is breathtaking. There is also the **Lower Story**. We live on earth. We make mistakes, run from God, and resist his overtures of love. Sometimes we get so mired in the Lower Story that we fail to recognize God's presence breaking into our world. We forget that the God of heaven longs to have a growing relationship, a friendship, with us—and ultimately sent his Son, Jesus, who died for our sins and rose again to restore that relationship for all who will believe. It is in *The Story of Heaven* that these two stories reach their glorious climax: when sin, death, and sorrow will be no more and God will be reunited with his people forever.

Exit Strategy

In life, the end is often exactly that, the end.
With Jesus, the end can become the beginning.

Bible Readings

Now a man named Lazarus was sick. He was from Bethany, the village of Mary and her sister Martha. (This Mary, whose brother Lazarus now lay sick, was the same one who poured perfume on the Lord and wiped his feet with her hair.) So the sisters sent word to Jesus, "Lord, the one you love is sick."

When he heard this, Jesus said, "This sickness will not end in death. No, it is for God's glory so that God's Son may be glorified through it." Now Jesus loved Martha and her sister and Lazarus. So when he heard that Lazarus was sick, he stayed where he was two more days, and then he said to his disciples, "Let us go back to Judea."

"But Rabbi," they said, "a short while ago the Jews there tried to stone you, and yet you are going back?"

Jesus answered, "Are there not twelve hours of daylight? Anyone who walks in the daytime will not stumble, for they see by this world's light. It is when a person walks at night that they stumble, for they have no light."

After he had said this, he went on to tell them, "Our friend Lazarus has fallen asleep; but I am going there to wake him up."

His disciples replied, "Lord, if he sleeps, he will get better." Jesus had been speaking of his death, but his disciples thought he meant natural sleep.

So then he told them plainly, "Lazarus is dead, and for your sake I am glad I was not there, so that you may believe. But let us go to him."

Then Thomas (also known as Didymus) said to the rest of the disciples, "Let us also go, that we may die with him."

On his arrival, Jesus found that Lazarus had already been in the tomb for four days. Now Bethany was less than two miles from Jerusalem, and many Jews had come to Martha and Mary to comfort them in the loss of their brother. When Martha heard that Jesus was coming, she went out to meet him, but Mary stayed at home.

"Lord," Martha said to Jesus, "if you had been here, my brother would not have died. But I know that even now God will give you whatever you ask."

Jesus said to her, "Your brother will rise again."

Martha answered, "I know he will rise again in the resurrection at the last day."

Jesus said to her, "I am the resurrection and the life. The one who believes in me will live, even though they die; and whoever lives by believing in me will never die. Do you believe this?"

"Yes, Lord," she replied, "I believe that you are the Messiah, the Son of God, who is to come into the world."

After she had said this, she went back and called her sister Mary aside. "The Teacher is here," she said, "and is asking for you." When Mary heard this, she got up quickly and went to him. Now Jesus had not yet entered the village, but was still at the place where Martha had met him. When the Jews who had been with Mary in the house, comforting her, noticed how quickly she got up and went out, they followed her, supposing she was going to the tomb to mourn there.

When Mary reached the place where Jesus was and saw him, she fell at his feet and said, "Lord, if you had been here, my brother would not have died."

When Jesus saw her weeping, and the Jews who had come along with her also weeping, he was deeply moved in spirit and troubled. "Where have you laid him?" he asked.

"Come and see, Lord," they replied.

Jesus wept.

Then the Jews said, "See how he loved him!"

But some of them said, "Could not he who opened the eyes of the blind man have kept this man from dying?"

Jesus, once more deeply moved, came to the tomb. It was a cave with a stone laid across the entrance. "Take away the stone," he said.

"But, Lord," said Martha, the sister of the dead man, "by this time there is a bad odor, for he has been there four days."

Then Jesus said, "Did I not tell you that if you believe, you will see the glory of God?"

So they took away the stone. Then Jesus looked up and said, "Father, I thank you that you have heard me. I knew that you always hear me, but I said this for the benefit of the people standing here, that they may believe that you sent me."

When he had said this, Jesus called in a loud voice, "Lazarus, come out!" The dead man came out, his hands and feet wrapped with strips of linen, and a cloth around his face.

Jesus said to them, "Take off the grave clothes and let him go."

John 11:1 – 44

Jesus took the Twelve aside and told them, "We are going up to Jerusalem, and everything that is written by the prophets about the Son of Man will be fulfilled. He will be delivered over to the Gentiles. They will mock him, insult him and spit on him; they will flog him and kill him. On the third day he will rise again."

Luke 18:31 – 33

[The disciples] were startled and frightened, thinking they saw a ghost. [Jesus] said to them, "Why are you troubled, and why do doubts rise in your minds? Look at my hands and my feet. It is I myself! Touch me and see; a ghost does not have flesh and bones, as you see I have."

When he had said this, he showed them his hands and feet. And while they still did not believe it because of joy and amazement, he asked them, "Do you have anything to eat?" They gave him a piece of broiled fish, and he took it and ate it in their presence.

He said to them, "This is what I told you while I was still with you: Everything must be fulfilled that is written about me in the Law of Moses, the Prophets and the Psalms."

Then he opened their minds so they could understand the Scriptures. He told them, "This is what is written: The Messiah will suffer and rise from the dead on the third day, and repentance for the forgiveness of sins will be preached in his name to all nations, beginning in Jerusalem."

Luke 24:37–47

Now, brothers and sisters, I [Paul] want to remind you of the gospel I preached to you, which you received and on which you have taken your stand. By this gospel you are saved, if you hold firmly to the word I preached to you. Otherwise, you have believed in vain.

For what I received I passed on to you as of first importance: that Christ died for our sins according to the Scriptures, that he was buried, that he was raised on the third day according to the Scriptures, and that he appeared to Cephas, and then to the Twelve. After that, he appeared to more than five hundred of the brothers and sisters at the same time, most of whom are still living, though some have fallen asleep.

But if it is preached that Christ has been raised from the dead, how can some of you say that there is no resurrection of the dead? If there is no resurrection of the dead, then not even Christ has been raised. And if Christ has not been raised, our preaching is useless and so is your faith. More than that, we are then found to be false witnesses about God, for we have testified about God that he raised Christ from the dead. But he did not raise him if in fact the dead are not raised. For if the dead are not raised, then Christ has not been raised either. And if Christ has not been raised, your faith is futile; you are still in your sins. Then those also who have fallen asleep in Christ are lost. If only for this life we have hope in Christ, we are of all people most to be pitied.

But Christ has indeed been raised from the dead, the firstfruits of those who have fallen asleep. For since death came through a man, the resurrection of the dead comes also through a man. For as in Adam all die, so in Christ all will be made alive. But each in turn: Christ, the firstfruits; then, when he comes, those who belong to him. Then the end will come, when he hands over the kingdom to God the Father after he has destroyed all dominion, authority and power. For he must reign until he has put all his enemies under his feet. The last enemy to be destroyed is death.

Listen, I tell you a mystery: We will not all sleep, but we will all be changed — in a flash, in the twinkling of an eye, at the last trumpet. For the trumpet will sound, the dead will be raised imperishable, and we will be changed. For the perishable must clothe itself with the imperishable, and the mortal with immortality. When the perishable has been clothed with the imperishable, and the mortal with immortality, then the saying that is written will come true: "Death has been swallowed up in victory."

"Where, O death, is your victory?

Where, O death, is your sting?"

The sting of death is sin, and the power of sin is the law. But thanks be to God! He gives us the victory through our Lord Jesus Christ.

Therefore, my dear brothers and sisters, stand firm. Let

nothing move you. Always give yourselves fully to the work of the Lord, because you know that your labor in the Lord is not in vain.

1 Corinthians 15:1 – 6, 12 – 26, 51 – 58

Study Guide

Introduction from the Video

Ralls, Texas, was a weathered tumbleweed of a town in 1965. The city center consisted of a two-story courthouse framed by a weedy lawn and bricked roads. One drugstore had gone out of business, and the second was not far behind. The closest resemblance to a traffic jam occurred every morning when farmers left the diner parking lot after their sunrise coffee.

It was as if someone had pressed the pause button and forgotten to release it. Which was just fine with my grandparents, God bless 'em. Charles and Macey McDermott looked just like the farm couple in Grant Wood's painting, only not nearly as energetic. Grandpa, lanky and long-faced; she, shorter and dark-eyed. Neither one smiled much. They shuffled about in a two-bedroom frame house, chewing Brown's Mule tobacco, watching soap operas, and reading Zane Grey novels.

It was my mom's idea for me to spend a week with them. Let ten-year-old Max get to know his grandparents' and mom's hometown. So she gave me a chocolate bar and a kiss, loaded me on a Greyhound bus, and waved goodbye.

The trip peaked with the candy bar. After one day I knew

this was going to be the longest week of my life. My grand-parents had no bicycles, baseballs, or basketball hoops. They knew no other ten-year-olds and lived too far out in the country for me to find any. Dullsville.

But then during lunch one day, I asked my grandmother about the photo that hung in her bedroom — the sepia-toned picture that was professionally taken and handsomely set in an oval-shaped walnut frame. Who was this mystery man who occupied prime real estate above my grandmother's bed?

"That's Levi Thornton," Grandma told me. "Your grand-father." I'd heard of this man. How he brought my mom to the farm country. How he died young. But where had he come from? How had he died? I didn't know.

So Grandma set out to tell me. Within a couple of sentences, I was lost in the story, bouncing in the cab of the 1929 Chevy pickup with Grandpa Levi, Grandma, and an eight-year-old version of my mom. I was happy to listen, and Grandma was thrilled to talk. For the better part of that day, we shinnied up the family tree and explored branches I had never known existed. As we did, my black-and-white week exploded into a Monet of colors.

Why do you suppose, now forty years removed, that I still remember the day in such detail? I still see the kitchen in which we sat, its straight-backed chairs and Formica-topped table. I see Grandma spilling photos out of a box and details out of her heart as if neither had been taken off the shelf in quite some time.

I recall an emotion similar to the one you likely felt when

you learned about your great-grandfather's migration from Norway or a distant relation being one of the charter Royal Canadian Mounties. Perhaps you've traced your ancestry through the Apache hunting grounds, African slave ships, or Polynesian sailors. We love to know where we came from.

And we *need* to know where we came from. Knowing connects us, links us, bonds us to something greater than we are. Knowing reminds us that we aren't floating on isolated ponds but on a grand river.

That's why God wants you to know his story. Framed photos hang in his house. Lively talks await you at his table. Stories about Bethlehem beginnings, enemy warfare in the wilderness, and fishermen friends in Galilee. The stumbles of Peter and the stubbornness of Paul. All a part of the story, but only subplots to the central message: "For God so loved the world that he gave his one and only Son, that whoever believes in him shall not perish but have eternal life" (John 3:16). This is the headline of the story: God saves his people!

The Bible says so. Scripture assures us of heaven. "Because Jesus was raised from the dead, we've been given a brand-new life and have everything to live for, including a future in heaven — and the future starts now!" (1 Peter 1:3 – 4 MSG).

Jesus says so. "He told them, 'This is what is written: The Christ will suffer and rise from the dead on the third day, and repentance and forgiveness of sins will be preached in his name to all nations, beginning at Jerusalem. You are witnesses of these things'" (Luke 24:46 – 48).

The angel says so. "The angel said to the women, 'Do not be afraid, for I know that you are looking for Jesus, who was crucified. He is not here; he has risen, just as he said. Come and see the place where he lay'" (Matthew 28:5 – 6).

Witnesses say so. "He was seen by Peter and then by the twelve apostles. After that, Jesus was seen by more than five hundred of the believers at the same time" (1 Corinthians 15:5 – 6 NCV).

Even the rolled-away stone testifies to Christ's rising from the dead (Matthew 28:1 – 7). No barrier will keep us locked inside the grave. Christ was the first example that we will all follow.

We all have a start date and an end date, known only by God before we were born. The clock began ticking the moment we were conceived in the womb. But as God's story of heaven reveals, we also have an exit strategy.

Talk About It

Tell about a time that a Christian family member or friend passed away. What feelings did you have during this season of loss and how did you experience both sorrow and joy?

Video Teaching Notes

As you watch the video teaching segment for session 1, featuring Max Lucado, use the following outline to record anything that stands out to you.

The folly of not having an exit strategy

No dream of a Sunday morning miracle

Plans to embalm Jesus, not talk to him

Cadaver turned King: he is risen!

The bodily resurrection of Jesus means everything

Promise about our grave

Death is not the final chapter

Video Discussion

NOTE: For your convenience, most of the Bible readings referenced in the following discussion questions are also found in the Bible Readings section at the beginning of this session, though sometimes the Bible Readings section versions are expanded.

1. In the video, Max said, "We all have a start date and an end date, known only by God before we were born. The clock began ticking the moment we were conceived in the womb." Despite this undeniable truth, why do you think so many people walk through this life failing to plan for their ultimate departure? What do Christians have to share with others that will help them get ready for the end of life on this planet?

2. Satan would love to keep every man, woman, and child so distracted and busy that they never face their own mortality and the reality that death looms in front of us all. What are some of the Enemy's distractions that keep people from asking important spiritual and eternal questions?

3. If a non-Christian friend or family member asked you, "What do you believe will happen to you when this life ends?" how would you explain eternity and your faith and confidence in God in a way that would make sense to them?

4. If a nonbelieving family member or friend was drawing near the end of their life and they asked you, "How can I prepare for eternity and to meet God?" what would you say to them? How would you help them prepare?

5. **Read:** Luke 18:31 – 33; 24:45 – 47. Imagine you were one of the disciples who walked with Jesus and heard him declare things like this with crystal clarity. How could they have heard these words and still not have realized that Jesus was actually going to rise again from the dead? Give examples of ways that we hear Jesus declare things with clarity and conviction but still don't fully embrace the truth of what he says.

6. In the video, Max talked about how the disciples got stuck on Saturday (Jesus' body in the tomb), but they needed to move into Sunday (Christ risen and alive!). How can Christians today get stuck on Saturday and forget that we live in the glorious victory of Resurrection Sunday? What can we do to inspire ourselves, and others, to live in the hope and reality of Easter Sunday?

The bodily resurrection means everything. If Jesus lives on only in spirit and deeds, he is but one of a thousand dead heroes. But if he lives on in flesh and bone, he is the King who pressed his heel against the head of death.
—Max Lucado

7. **Read:** 1 Corinthians 15:12 – 18. Why is absolute confidence in the bodily resurrection of Jesus so critical to the Christian faith? According to the apostle Paul, what are the implications for us if Christ has not risen from the dead?

8. **Read:** 1 Corinthians 15:51 – 58. How does the resurrection of Jesus and our assurance of eternal life, through faith in his name, impact our lives today and forever?

9. **Read:** John 11:17 – 27. How does Jesus connect his resurrection and the eternal condition of those who have faith in him? If we believe these words of Jesus, how should our assurance of eternal life impact the way we live today?

> *What Jesus did with his own grave,*
> *he promises to do with yours: empty it.*
> —Max Lucado

10. When we are assured of Jesus' resurrection and confident that heaven is our home, everything changes. What transformation have you experienced in *one* of these areas as you have grown more and more confident that the final chapter of your life is really just a preface to eternity with God?

   • How you view this life and the way you invest your time ...

   • How you share God's love and message of grace with others ...

- How you use your resources and the way you view material things ...
- How you view and treat people who have not yet entered a saving relationship with Jesus ...
- Some other area of your life ...

Which one of these areas would you desire to grow in and how can your small group members pray for you as you journey forward?

Closing Prayer

Take time as a group to pray in some of the following directions:

- Thank Jesus for his sacrificial death in your place on the cross ... to deal with all your sins. And thank him for his glorious resurrection and the certainty you have that heaven will be your home because he has opened and prepared the way!

- Pray for people you love and care about who have still not embraced God's plan for their life and eternity.

- Confess where you get stuck on Saturday and forget to celebrate the joy and confidence that come in knowing that Sunday has come and Jesus has risen.

- Ask God to help you walk in the resurrection power of Jesus each and every day of your life.

Between Sessions

Personal Reflection

Read: 1 Corinthians 15. Reflect on the importance of Jesus' resurrection — to you personally and on a broader level. What would be different if Jesus had not risen? How has hope invaded our world through the resurrection? What do you have to look forward to because Jesus rose from the dead and you have received his grace?

Personal Action

So many people have no "exit strategy" from this world. They are caught up in the distractions and stuff of life and don't think past the next week or month. Commit to pray for family and friends who have not entered a life-saving friendship with Jesus. Ask God to give you opportunities to move from prayer into action as you share with others what the resurrection of Jesus means to you and what it could mean in their life ... and eternity.

Read for Next Session

Take time before your next small group to read the Bible Readings for session 2, "Heavenly Graduation." Also go back and read the session 1 Bible Readings if you haven't already.

REFLECTIONS AND NOTES

_____

_____

_____

_____

_____

_____

_____

_____

_____

_____

_____

_____

_____

_____

_____

_____

_____

_____

_____

_____

_____

_____

Heavenly Graduation

*We cling tightly to this life,
but for followers of Jesus,
the best is yet to come!*

Bible Readings

[Jesus said,] "Do not let your hearts be troubled. You believe in God, believe also in me. My Father's house has many rooms; if that were not so, would I have told you that I am going there to prepare a place for you? And if I go and prepare a place for you, I will come back and take you to be with me that you also may be where I am. You know the way to the place where I am going."

John 14:1 – 4

But someone will ask, "How are the dead raised? With what kind of body will they come?" How foolish! How you sow does not come to life unless it dies. When you sow, you do not plant the body that will be, but just a seed, perhaps of wheat or of something else. But God gives it a body as he has determined, and to each kind of seed he gives its own body. Not all flesh is the same: People have one kind of flesh, animals have another, birds another and fish another. There are also heavenly bodies and there are earthly bodies; but the splendor of the heavenly bodies is one kind, and the splendor of the earthly bodies is another. The sun has one kind of splendor, the moon another and the stars another; and star differs from star in splendor.

So it will be with the resurrection of the dead. The body that is sown perishable, it is raised imperishable; it is sown in dishonor, it is raised in glory; it is sown in weakness, it is raised in power; it is sown a natural body, it is raised a spiritual body.

1 Corinthians 15:35 – 44

We know that the one who raised the Lord Jesus from the dead will also raise us with Jesus ... Therefore we do not lose heart. Though outwardly we are wasting away, yet inwardly we are being renewed day by day. For our light and momentary troubles are achieving for us an eternal glory that far outweighs them all. So we fix our eyes not on what is seen, but on what is unseen, since what is seen is temporary, but what is unseen is eternal.

For we know that if the earthly tent we live in is destroyed, we have a building from God, an eternal house in heaven, not built by human hands. Meanwhile we groan, longing to be clothed instead with our heavenly dwelling, because when we are clothed, we will not be found naked. For while we are in this tent, we groan and are burdened, because we do not wish to be unclothed but to be clothed instead with our heavenly dwelling, so that what is mortal may be swallowed up by life. Now the one who has fashioned us for this very purpose is God, who has given us the Spirit as a deposit, guaranteeing what is to come.

Therefore we are always confident and know that as long as we are at home in the body we are away from the Lord. For we live by faith, not by sight. We are confident, I say, and would prefer to be away from the body and at home with the Lord. So we make it our goal to please him whether we are at home in the body or away from it. For we must all appear before the judgment seat of Christ, so that each of us may receive what is due us for the things done while in the body, whether good or bad.

2 Corinthians 4:14, 16 – 18; 5:1 – 10

Brothers and sisters, we do not want you to be uninformed about those who sleep in death, so that you do not grieve like the rest of mankind, who have no hope. For we believe that Jesus died and rose again, and so we believe that God will bring with Jesus those who have fallen asleep in him. According to the Lord's word, we tell you that we who are still alive, who are left until the coming of the Lord, will certainly not precede those who have fallen asleep. For the Lord himself will come down from heaven, with a loud command, with the voice of the archangel and with the trumpet call of God, and the dead in Christ will rise first. After that, we who are still alive and are left will be caught up together with them in the clouds to meet the Lord in the air. And so we will be with the Lord forever. Therefore encourage one another with these words. *1509*

1 Thessalonians 4:13 – 18

See what great love the Father has lavished on us, that we should be called children of God! And that is what we are! The reason the world does not know us is that it did not know him. Dear friends, now we are children of God, and what we will be has not yet been made known. But we know that when Christ appears, we shall be like him, for we shall see him as he is. All who have this hope in him purify themselves, just as he is pure.

1 John 1:1 – 3

Then the angel showed me the river of the water of life, as clear as crystal, flowing from the throne of God and of the Lamb down the middle of the great street of the city. On each side of the river stood the tree of life, bearing twelve crops of fruit, yielding its fruit every month. And the leaves of the tree are for the healing of the nations. No longer will there be any curse. The throne of God and of the Lamb will be in the city, and his servants will serve him.   *1667*

Revelation 22:1 – 3

Return to paradise
1668

Study Guide

Introduction from the Video

For all we don't know about Mr. Holden Howie, of one thing we can be certain. He knew his birds would find their way home.

Several times a day the square-bodied, gray-bearded New Zealander retrieved one of his pigeons from his Auckland aviary. Securing the feathered courier with one hand, he attached the correspondence with the other. Some birds carried as many as five messages at a time. Mr. Howie released the bird into the South Pacific sky, and it flew as straight as string to its nest on Great Barrier Island.

Between 1898 and 1908, Mr. Howie delivered thousands of messages this way between Auckland and Great Barrier Island. His birds were speedy. They could travel in two hours the distance a boat would traverse in three days. Dependable. Storms rarely knocked the pigeons off course, and they never called in sick. And, most notably, they were accurate. They could find their nest. After all, why else would we call them homing pigeons?

Other birds fly faster. Other birds are stronger. Other birds boast larger plumes or stronger claws. But none have the navigational skill of the homing pigeon.

Some scientists believe pigeons have traces of magnetite in their beaks and brains that interplay with the magnetic field of the earth. Others credit the birds' sense of hearing. Do they pick up a frequency other birds miss? Or do they sniff out their target with a keen sense of smell?

We don't know for sure, but what we do know is this: pigeons have an innate home detector. So do you. What God gave to pigeons he also gave to you. No, not bird brains. A guidance system. You were born heaven-equipped with a hunger for your heavenly home.

Need proof? Think about the questions we ask. Questions about death and time, significance and relevance. How did we get here? What are we here for? Are we someone's idea or something's accident? Why on earth are we on this earth? Animals don't ask the questions we do. Dogs howl at the moon, but we stare at it and wonder.

We ask questions about pain and why the words "leukemia" and "child" often appear in the same sentence. We ask questions about war and why conflict can't go the way of phonograph records and telegrams. We ask questions about the grave and why the dash between the dates on a tombstone is so small. Something tells us this isn't right, good, fair. Something tells us this isn't home.

The Bible states that "God ... has planted eternity in the human heart" (Ecclesiastes 3:11 NLT). Just as Mr. Howie released his pigeons for Auckland, God has released his children from the cage of time. Our privilege is to keep flapping until we spot the island — until we graduate from this life into the next. Those who do will discover a spiritual cache, a treasure hidden in a field, a pearl of great value.

In God's story of heaven, life on earth is but the beginning — the first letter of the first sentence in the first chapter of the great story God is writing with your life.

As King David discovered, "God rewrote the text of my life when I opened the book of my heart to his eyes" (2 Samuel 22:25 MSG). But what is the text of our lives?

The question is not a new one. Self-help gurus, talk-show hosts, and magazine headlines urge you to find your narrative. But they send you in the wrong direction. "Look inside yourself," they say. But the promise of self-discovery falls short. Can you find the plot of a book in one paragraph or hear the flow of a symphony in one measure? Can you uncover the plot of your life by examining your life? By no means.

You are so much more than a few days between the womb and the tomb.

Your story indwells God's. This is the great promise of the Bible. "It's in Christ that we find out who we are and what we are living for. Long before we first heard of Christ and got our hopes up, he had his eye on us, had designs on us for glorious living, part of the overall purpose he is working out in everything and everyone" (Ephesians 1:11 – 12 MSG).

Above and around us God directs a grander saga, written by his hand, orchestrated by his will, unveiled according to his calendar. And you are a part of it. Your life emerges from the greatest mind and the kindest heart in the history of the universe: the mind and heart of God. "He makes everything work out according to his plan" (v. 11 NLT).

Talk About It

Tell about a time you tried a new product with high hopes and expectations only to end up discouraged and disheartened when the advertising promises did not match your reality.

Video Teaching Notes

As you watch the video teaching segment for session 2, featuring Max Lucado, use the following outline to record anything that stands out to you.

Graduation is no small matter

God will reunite your body with your soul

All things in Christ

Sigh of sadness in suffering

Jesus heals

We shall be like Jesus

No more curse

How to live these days on earth

Video Discussion

NOTE: For your convenience, most of the Bible readings referenced in the following discussion questions are also found in the Bible Readings section at the beginning of this session, though sometimes the Bible Readings section versions are expanded.

1. In the video, Max talked about how we are all born with a hunger for our heavenly home. How is the day a Christian dies really a homecoming or graduation day? What are we graduating from and what are we graduating to?

Earthly life – Eternal life

2. **Read:** 1 Corinthians 15:35 – 44. One promise God makes is that when this life ends, we will receive a new and eternal body. How will our new spiritual bodies be an upgrade compared to the ones we have right now? What is one thing that excites you about receiving a new and spiritual body?

p. 1532 - 33

all will be healed

1589 - Bodies - not just Spiritual bodies

3. **Read:** Mark 7:31 – 35. Jesus did a lot of healing while he was on this earth. As you look at this account and others recorded in the four Gospels (Matthew, Mark, Luke, and John), what do you learn about how Jesus healed? What do you learn about why Jesus healed people?

When asked / no personal praise
"Everyday" people
people He loved - Lazarus
children
He healed thru God given power
Gave His gift to disciples

4. We know that when this life ends and we graduate, we will receive new bodies. Until then, the Bible tells us that we can and should pray for healing for those who are sick and face physical struggles (James 5:13 – 16). Who are you praying for right now and how can your group members join you in both praying for and caring for these people?

> I hate disease.
> I'm sick of it.
> So is Christ.
> —Max Lucado

5. **Read:** 1 John 3:1 – 3. What do you learn about God in this passage? What do you learn about yourself?

6. First John 3:2 assures us that one day (postgraduation), "We shall be like him." In what ways are we already becoming more like Jesus? In what ways will we be even more like Jesus after our final graduation day? In what ways will Jesus always be unique and different from us?

7. **Read:** Romans 7:15 – 19. The apostle Paul is brutally honest about the struggle we all face with sin in this life. What does Paul say about our battle with sin and how do his words resonate with your experience?

8. In light of what the apostle Paul teaches in Romans 7, what is one thing you really want to do, but find it difficult to follow through on?

   What is one thing you find yourself doing, but you hate it and want to stop? How can your group pray for you and keep you accountable in these areas of your life?

9. **Read:** Revelation 22:1 – 3. After our graduation day, the curse of sin will be gone. How does this promise give hope in this life? What are some sins and struggles that you look forward to dismissing?

Heaven has scheduled a graduation. Sin will no longer be at war with our flesh. Eyes won't lust, thoughts won't wander, hands won't steal, our minds won't judge, appetites won't rage, and our tongues won't lie. We will be brand-new.
—Max Lucado

---

10. **Read:** 2 Corinthians 4:16 – 18 and Romans 8:18. How does the apostle Paul compare this life to the life to come? How can a passage like this help us when we face pain, struggles, and loss?

Why is meditating on heaven and remembering what comes after graduation day so important for Christians?

Closing Prayer

Take time as a group to pray in some of the following directions:

- Thank God that heaven really is your home and that Jesus has already gone ahead of you to prepare the way.

- Tell God of your heartache concerning the pain and struggles of this world. Pray for his compassion to fill your heart so that you can help bring his grace, love, and comfort to those who are hurting.

- Lift up people you care about who are facing physical ailments and challenges. Ask for the grace of God, his comfort, and his healing touch to be upon them.

- Thank God for the people you love who have gone before you to heaven. Praise God that they were part of your life for a season and that they are with Jesus now.

Between Sessions

Personal Reflection

One day the curse of sin will be gone (Revelation 22:3), but until our final graduation we will do battle with it. This week identify two or three areas of temptation with which the Enemy tries to lure you. Then do three things: (1) pray for power to overcome and eyes to see the tactics of the Enemy; (2) take practical steps to avoid places and situations that would open the door to possible temptation in these areas of struggle; (3) invite a trusted member of your small group to pray for you and keep you accountable to walk in holiness in these areas.

Personal Action

Make a list of people you care about who are dealing with physical ailments and ongoing health issues. Commit to pray for them on a weekly basis. As circumstances permit, give them an occasional call and pray with them over the phone, or meet with them for prayer. When God answers prayers for healing, praise him and give him the glory. When there is no healing, continue praying and place your trust in God's sovereign power and wisdom.

Read for Next Session

Take time before your next small group to read the Bible Readings for session 3, "The End of Time." Also go back and read the session 2 Bible Readings if you haven't already.

REFLECTIONS AND NOTES

_____

_____

_____

_____

_____

_____

_____

_____

_____

_____

_____

_____

_____

_____

_____

_____

_____

_____

_____

_____

_____

_____

_____

The End of Time

God wins!
If we are on his side,
we win too.

Bible Readings

John,

To the seven churches in the province of Asia:

Grace and peace to you from him who is, and who was, and who is to come, and from the seven spirits before his throne, and from Jesus Christ, who is the faithful witness, the firstborn from the dead, and the ruler of the kings of the earth.

To him who loves us and has freed us from our sins by his blood, and has made us to be a kingdom and priests to serve his God and Father — to him be glory and power for ever and ever! Amen.

"Look, he is coming with the clouds,"
        and "every eye will see him,
even those who pierced him";
        and all peoples on earth "will mourn because of him."

So shall it be! Amen.

"I am the Alpha and the Omega," says the Lord God, "who is, and who was, and who is to come, the Almighty."

Revelation 1:4 – 8

Then I saw in the right hand of him who sat on the throne a scroll with writing on both sides and sealed with seven seals. And I saw a mighty angel proclaiming in a loud voice, "Who is worthy to break the seals and open the scroll?" But no one in heaven or on earth or under the earth could open the scroll or even look inside it. I wept and wept because no one was found who was worthy to open the scroll or look inside. Then one of the elders said to me, "Do not weep! See, the Lion of the tribe of Judah, the Root of David, has triumphed. He is able to open the scroll and its seven seals."

Then I saw a Lamb, looking as if it had been slain, standing at the center of the throne, encircled by the four living creatures and the elders. The Lamb had seven horns and seven eyes, which are the seven spirits of God sent out into all the earth. He went and took the scroll from the right hand of him who sat on the throne. And when he had taken it, the four living creatures and the twenty-four elders fell down before the Lamb. Each one had a harp and they were holding golden bowls full of incense, which are the prayers of God's people. And they sang a new song, saying:

"You are worthy to take the scroll
      and to open its seals,
   because you were slain,
      and with your blood you purchased for God
      persons from every tribe and language and people
            and nation.
You have made them to be a kingdom and priests
            to serve our God,
      and they will reign on the earth."

Then I looked and heard the voice of many angels, numbering thousands upon thousands, and ten thousand times ten thousand. They encircled the throne and the living creatures and the elders. In a loud voice they were saying:

"Worthy is the Lamb, who was slain,
   to receive power and wealth and wisdom and
   strength
   and honor and glory and praise!"

Then I heard every creature in heaven and on earth and under the earth and on the sea, and all that is in them, saying:

"To him who sits on the throne and to the Lamb
   be praise and honor and glory and power,
for ever and ever!"

The four living creatures said, "Amen," and the elders fell down and worshiped.

Revelation 5

Then I saw "a new heaven and a new earth," for the first heaven and the first earth had passed away, and there was no longer any sea. I saw the Holy City, the new Jerusalem, coming down out of heaven from God, prepared as a bride beautifully dressed for her husband. And I heard a loud voice from the throne saying, "Look! God's dwelling place is now among the people, and he will dwell with them. They will be his people, and God himself will be with them and be their God. 'He will wipe every tear from their eyes. There will be no more death' or mourning or crying or pain, for the old order of things has passed away."

He who was seated on the throne said, "I am making

everything new!" Then he said, "Write this down, for these words are trustworthy and true."

He said to me: "It is done. I am the Alpha and the Omega, the Beginning and the End. To the thirsty I will give water without cost from the spring of the water of life. Those who are victorious will inherit all this, and I will be their God and they will be my children. But the cowardly, the unbelieving, the vile, the murderers, the sexually immoral, those who practice magic arts, the idolaters and all liars — they will be consigned to the fiery lake of burning sulfur. This is the second death."

One of the seven angels who had the seven bowls full of the seven last plagues came and said to me, "Come, I will show you the bride, the wife of the Lamb." And he carried me away in the Spirit to a mountain great and high, and showed me the Holy City, Jerusalem, coming down out of heaven from God. It shone with the glory of God, and its brilliance was like that of a very precious jewel, like a jasper, clear as crystal. It had a great, high wall with twelve gates, and with twelve angels at the gates. On the gates were written the names of the twelve tribes of Israel. There were three gates on the east, three on the north, three on the south and three on the west. The wall of the city had twelve foundations, and on them were the names of the twelve apostles of the Lamb.

The angel who talked with me had a measuring rod of gold to measure the city, its gates and its walls. The city was laid out like a square, as long as it was wide. He measured the city with the rod and found it to be 12,000 stadia in length, and as wide and high as it is long. The angel measured the wall using human measurement, and it was 144 cubits thick. The wall was made of jasper, and the city of pure gold, as pure as glass. The foundations of the city walls were decorated with every kind of precious stone. The first foundation was jasper, the second sapphire, the third agate, the fourth emerald, the fifth onyx, the sixth ruby, the seventh chrysolite, the eighth beryl, the ninth topaz, the tenth turquoise, the eleventh jacinth, and the twelfth amethyst. The twelve gates were twelve pearls, each gate made of a single pearl. The great street of the city was of gold, as pure as transparent glass.

I did not see a temple in the city, because the Lord God Almighty and the Lamb are its temple. The city does not need the sun or the moon to shine on it, for the glory of God gives it light, and the Lamb is its lamp. The nations will walk by its light, and the kings of the earth will bring their splendor into it. On no day will its gates ever be shut, for there will be no night there. The glory and honor of the nations will be brought into it. Nothing impure will ever enter it, nor will anyone who does what is shameful or deceitful, but only those whose names are written in the Lamb's book of life.

Revelation 21

"Look, I am coming soon! My reward is with me, and I will give to each person according to what they have done. I am the Alpha and the Omega, the First and the Last, the Beginning and the End.

"Blessed are those who wash their robes, that they may have the right to the tree of life and may go through the gates into the city. Outside are the dogs, those who practice magic arts, the sexually immoral, the murderers, the idolaters and everyone who loves and practices falsehood.

"I, Jesus, have sent my angel to give you this testimony for the churches. I am the Root and the Offspring of David, and the bright Morning Star."

The Spirit and the bride say, "Come!" And let the one who hears say, "Come!" Let the one who is thirsty come; and let the one who wishes take the free gift of the water of life.

I warn everyone who hears the words of the prophecy of this scroll: If anyone adds anything to them, God will add to that person the plagues described in this scroll. And if anyone takes words away from this scroll of prophecy, God will take away from that person any share in the tree of life and in the Holy City, which are described in this scroll.

He who testifies to these things says, "Yes, I am coming soon."

Amen. Come, Lord Jesus.

The grace of the Lord Jesus be with God's people. Amen.

Revelation 22:12 – 21

Study Guide

Introduction from the Video

Growing up, my mother loved and sacrificed so much for my three siblings and me. She spent all of her money and time on us. So, several years ago when I was finally at a place in my life where I had a little financial margin, I called my mother to tell her that the day after Christmas, I was taking her and my dad on an all-expense paid trip to the magnificent Niagara Falls. I reserved rooms in a turn-of-the-century opulent hotel on the Canadian side facing the falls.

However, when I called my mother, she told me she wasn't feeling well. Initially, I thought she was just trying to wiggle out of the trip. But as the next few months unfolded and her illness got worse, I really started to worry. I decided to fly back to my parents' home a few days ahead of my family — a week before the trip.

Three days later, my mother died of advanced pancreatic cancer. The trip was cancelled just *three days* before we were scheduled to take off. Here I was finally in a place to do something for my mother, and I had missed it forever by three days! I was devastated on a number of levels.

This all happened during a time in my life as a pastor when two incredible men were mentoring me on growing in the Christian life: Dr. Dallas Willard and Dr. J. I. Packer. Both men challenged me on the same spiritual principle — that God didn't want me to believe his Word as just the right answer, but as a way of life.

The sudden death of my mother at the age of sixty-two caused me to face this operating principle for living head on. In a moment soaked in tears, I whispered honestly to God, "I don't believe in heaven!" Oh, I knew that believing in heaven was the "right answer."

I had taught on heaven in dozens of sermons and at hundreds of funerals. But deep in my heart, I just couldn't wrap my arms around such a fantastic idea. I wanted it to be true. I just didn't live as though it were.

If you have ever been through the loss of someone you loved, you have had to face this same principle for living. As you stood by the graveside of someone you loved — someone who belonged to God — you likely also struggled with wrapping your mind around the idea of heaven. You recalled memories of that person — the good times you shared or the tough times you faced together — but you were left with the empty feeling that the person was gone and there was nothing you could do to bring him or her back. It felt as if the relationship was over, and you wondered if there really was a place called heaven where you would meet that person again.

God knows that we struggle to understand concepts such as eternal life. He knows what our existence is like on earth. In the here and now of our daily lives — what we could call our "Lower Story" — we are focused on things such as making money, paying bills, dealing with sickness and breakups, working through conflicts, and coping with the death of loved ones. These are the story elements that concern us and occupy our minds, and as people of faith we trust God to meet our needs. And he does! He meets us and offers us wisdom and guidance on getting through life with dignity and purpose. He intervenes and applies healing salve to our physical and emotional wounds. Like a tenderhearted Father, God lavishes us with his care, stretching out his arms to comfort us when we are in distress and encourage us when we are down.

But when we are able to rise above the here and now and look beyond the daily grind of our lives, we see that God has a higher agenda than merely our survival and comfort.

We see that he has been up to something amazing from the very beginning of time. He has been writing an "Upper Story," and this story is infinitely more magnificent than any single chapter in our lives. We see that heaven is real and that Jesus' words are true when he promised that he would go and prepare a place for us there.

In my own life, after diving into what the Bible actually said about heaven and eternity, I discovered so many things that I didn't understand or see before. I realized that heaven is not about floating on clouds in outer space as spirit beings with angel's wings, singing songs and playing a harp 24/7. I discovered that God is going to make a new earth and come down into a beautiful garden, just like he did in the beginning, and that he is going to take walks with us in our new real-life bodies with skin on them. I also discovered that in the middle of the garden there is a "river of the water of life, as clear as crystal, flowing from the throne of God and of the Lamb down the middle of the great street of the city."

I figure this river will definitely rival the Niagara Falls. As it turns out, the trip with my mom has not been cancelled, just postponed. And the trip has been paid in full — not by her son, but by God's Son.

Over the last few years, I have been on a journey in the Lower Story, desperately trying to connect with God's Upper Story and his promise of eternal life. Today, I can say honestly that I believe in heaven, not just as the "right answer" but also as a way of life. This truth has filled me with hope and anticipation for the future walk with my mother and my God along the heavenly river.

Talk About It

Tell about the ending of one of your favorite books or children's stories. Why do you like this ending?

Video Teaching Notes

As you watch the video teaching segment for session 3, featuring Randy Frazee, use the following outline to record anything that stands out to you.

John's vision

No more tears

"Trees of life"

God's Upper Story vision is completely restored

Video Discussion

NOTE: For your convenience, most of the Bible readings referenced in the following discussion questions are also found in the Bible Readings section at the beginning of this session, though sometimes the Bible Readings section versions are expanded.

1. **Read:** Revelation 1:4–8 in which the apostle John paints an amazing picture of Jesus. According to this portrait, who is Jesus and what has he done?

2. The book of Revelation includes short letters written to seven real churches in the ancient world. **Read:** Revelation 2:1 – 7, Jesus' letter to the church in Ephesus. What did this letter to that congregation say regarding the following:

• What they were doing well

• Where they needed to grow or change

• What action they should take

3. What are specific ways we can make sure that Jesus remains the first love of our life and the first love in the life of the local church?

4. **Read:** Revelation 3:14 – 21, the letter to the church in Laodicea. Jesus told the people he did not want them to be "lukewarm." What does it look like when the church becomes lukewarm and what can we do to make sure our church stays hot for God?

5. **Read:** Revelation 5:11 – 21. In John's vision, he got glimpses of heavenly worship. What from these scenes do you learn about worship and how might this shape the way we engage and enter into praise of our God?

6. It is a serious and sobering reality that all people will spend eternity in heaven or hell. How does the book of Revelation (see 20:11 – 15) affirm this reality and how should this spur us to share the message and love of Jesus with the people in our life?

7. **Read:** Revelation 21:1 – 4, 22 – 27, a portion of John's description of what heaven will be like. What specific element of this vision makes you excited to spend eternity in this glorious place?

Revelation, the last book of the Bible, has sparked so much hope in believers throughout the ages. It keeps us going in the darkest of times. Regardless of how difficult life may be in the moment, we have, through Christ's sacrifice, this wonderful place to look forward to.
−Randy Frazee

8. In the video, Randy talked about how the hope of heaven touches his heart because he knows he will see his mom again, and they can worship Jesus together. Name one person you love who is already with Jesus. How does the hope of seeing this person again make heaven even more wonderful?

9. The culmination of God's marvelous story is this: God will be with his people again — forever. This has been his goal ever since mankind's fall in Eden. This life is really a time to practice for heaven. What can you do on a daily basis to stay close to God and have a dynamic friendship with him?

> *The Story comes to an end.*
> *But it's really the*
> *beginning.*
> –Randy Frazee

Closing Prayer

Take time as a group to pray in some of the following directions:

- Celebrate the glory and majesty of Jesus, the First and Last, the Alpha and Omega, the Lamb of God slain before the foundation of the world.

- Thank God that you know the rest of the story and that you are confident that God wins!

- Pray for power to stand strong in faith until he calls you to heaven or comes again.

In the Coming Days

Personal Reflections

Think back over your three-week journey through *The Story of Heaven* and reflect on all you have learned. You might want to look back over any notes you have jotted down in this study guide or reread any or all of the Bible Readings. Thank God, over and over again, for the promise of heaven and recommit yourself to living faithfully for him till you see him face to face!

Personal Action

Many people in our culture are fascinated with theories about the afterlife and heaven, as evidenced by the numerous magazine articles, books, and films that focus on these topics. Many are also fearful of death. Find a few men and women who you think might benefit from the truths presented in *The Story of Heaven* curriculum and (perhaps with some members of your current small group), offer to lead a study. As you have learned to see the big picture of God's love and activity in human history, share this gift with others.

REFLECTIONS AND NOTES

The Story of Jesus Participant's Guide with DVD

Experience the Life of Jesus as One Seamless Story

Randy Frazee
with Kevin and Sherry Harney

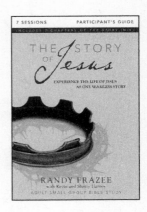

The Story of Jesus small group Bible study is a seven-week exploration of the life and ministry of Jesus. Adapted from the original *The Story Adult Curriculum*, it also includes the seven chapters of the *The Story* (NIV) that covers from the birth of Jesus to the birth of the church.

Through the seven video sessions, pastor and author Randy Frazee will open your eyes to the Lower Story, our story, which is actually many stories of men and women interacting with God in the daily course of life; and the Upper Story, which is the tale of his great, overarching purpose that fits all the individual stories together like panels in one unified mural.

The Story of Jesus Participant's Guide includes video teaching notes, discussion questions, and between-session personal experiences to help you know the joy that comes as you align your story with Jesus' story.

Available in stores and online!

Surprised by Hope Participant's Guide with DVD

Rethinking Heaven, the Resurrection, and the Mission of the Church

N. T. Wright

Many Christians believe our future in heaven is all that really matters. But that's not what the Bible teaches. Through this small group Bible study, premier Bible scholar N. T. Wright brings you inside the Scriptures to grasp the full, breathtaking hope Jesus offers the world, and its implications for your life today.

In six transforming, faith-inspiring video sessions, N. T. Wright opens your eyes what God's Word has to say about the world to come and the world that is.

Explore such questions as: What is heaven really like? Is our main duty as Christians simply to help non-Christians get there? What hope does the gospel hold for this present life? In what ways does God intend for us to experience that hope personally and spread its healing power to the world around us? *Surprised by Hope* provides a clearer vision both of the future and of God's kingdom at hand today.

Sessions include:

1. Hope for the World
2. The Hope of the Resurrection
3. The Hope of Heaven
4. The Hope of Jesus' Second Coming
5. The Hope of Salvation
6. The Hope of the Church

Available in stores and online!